REVEREND
GERALD P. RUANE, PH.D.

The Greatest Healing Gifts

VOLUME I.—
THE EUCHARIST

ACKNOWLEDGEMENTS

Special and sincerest thanks to the many people who have taught me about Jesus Christ in the Eucharist. My family — parents and siblings and now their families — has encouraged and enlightened me by their faith and love for the Lord.

The people of the Sacred Heart Institute and of the parishes and institutions where I have served have blessed me with their fervent participation at weekday and Sunday celebrations and at Healing Masses celebrated throughout New Jersey, the U.S., and abroad.

In particular I owe an enormous debt of gratitude to Sister Ruthann Williams, O.P., administrator of the Sacred Heart Institute, who is a multi-talented woman. Her artistic and literary abilities and her wizardry with the word processor have helped me immensely.

Ed and Agnes Kardauskas supported our efforts and were their usual superb selves as proofreaders and in many other capacities.

GPR

DEDICATION

This volume is about

Jesus Christ

our Eucharistic Lord and Healer

I dedicate it to Him Who alone will
make these words touch the hearts and minds
of his people, and to

His Blessed Mother
under the title of
Our Lady of the Blessed Sacrament

THE GREATEST HEALING GIFTS

Volume I

THE EUCHARIST

Contents

i

ANIMA CHRISTI

Soul of Christ, sanctify me.
Body of Christ, save me.
Blood of Christ, exhilarate me.
Water from the side of Christ, wash me.
Passion of Christ, strengthen me.

PREFACE

Jesus Christ is the Greatest Healing Gift we have or will ever have. Consequently, he is too vast a Lord, a person, and a subject to understand in one thin volume. We will do so in a series of volumes.

This newest series of Institute books is entitled <u>The Greatest Healing Gifts</u>.

Volume I considers Jesus, our healer in and at the Eucharist.
Volume II will examine Jesus, the healing Word of the Sacred Scriptures.
Volume III will discuss how Jesus heals us through our devotion (hopefully on a daily basis) to our one God, Father, Son, and Holy Spirit; to the Blessed Virgin Mary; and to the angels and also the saints - living in heaven or on earth.

The magnificent Jersey shore has been the site for most of my writing on healing. I find its unique combination of sun, sand, and surf plus the large dining table in our family's home an unbeatable spur to my creative and literary juices.

May you be blessed with warm and sunny surroundings as you read this volume no matter what the weather is outside. Someone has said, "God lives in Southern California." He certainly does. But he lives everyplace. What's more important for us, God lives in you and in me. May his presence be especially real to you now as you begin to read about, and hopefully to understand more fully God's greatest healing gift to us: Jesus Christ.

Please Note

In this book I deliberately use words about the topic interchangeably. The Eucharist, Mass, Eucharistic Celebration, the Sacrifice of the Mass, the Lord's Supper, and the Banquet of the Lord are all words which describe what we are discussing. These terms each seek to describe a certain facet of our experience as Church. They have a long and venerable tradition in our Church. Use whatever one appeals to you, but always be open to what the others seek to highlight.

CHAPTER ONE

PERSONAL REFLECTIONS

Jesus is the greatest Healing Gift and in the Eucharist he is present to each and every Catholic-Christian in a special way. "Special" is such a poor word for the Eucharistic presence of Jesus Christ, but let's use it for now. If we are faithful in our quest to understand this greatest of all healing gifts, many other words will spring to life in our minds and hearts.

Write those words in the margin as they come to your mind because I sincerely request that you use this volume as a workbook. Underline and cross out what you want. Argue and discuss your ideas with me. No violence, please!

Take what you can accept now and make it your own. Leave the rest for later, but be open to the possibility that it might be helpful at some future date.

Don't share this book with another! Make it so personal by your notes and comments that you'll want to keep it. That's an excellent way to grow in God's healing love. The other person can buy his/her own copy and hopefully use it the same way. That will help him or her. (It will also boost sales which helps the Institute.)

May I begin with some personal reflections? Perhaps they will stir some memories hidden deep within you. At least, they will let you know why the Eucharist is so very meaningful to me.

Jesus in the Eucharist has touched me and entered most forcefully into my life. People often ask: "Why did you become a priest?" I've thought about that question often. The single most important influence was the Eucharist which drew me gently, but inevitably toward the priesthood.

Baptism Was Not
My Finest Performance

I always loved the Church but did not always behave with due reverence and respect. I was born early on a Saturday morning, January 6, and I was baptized that Sunday afternoon. No tremendous medical emergency, but my parents were Irish Catholics from Scranton, Pennsylvania. Their idea seemed to be "get him to the church on time."

Oddly enough, I don't remember much of that sacramental experience. However, others do; and the events of that day are

4

often recounted at family gatherings. You see, I cried through the whole thing. My Uncle Matt, my godfather and a great cigar smoker, used to say that the biggest temptation he had at the time was to jam one of his cigars into my mouth.

On the surface that Baptism, though valid, was not a scintillating liturgical triumph because there were several other babies who joined my infant rendering (or rending) of Gregorian chant.

However, our faith tells us that at Baptism Jesus touches us deeply and completely, no matter how loudly we protest. Or maybe we were professing and confessing our allegiance to him in our own way. After baptism we start to live out what has happened to us. We begin to understand who we are and especially <u>whose</u> we are. We begin to realize what things are important. What I am saying is that underneath the surface noise, clamor, or whatever, the Lord did claim me and mark me. So as a marked human being, sealed in a special way, I had his promise to lead me and he has continued to do so.

The Magnet Of Daily Mass

Actually, when I was in the 7th and 8th grades, I felt drawn to go to Mass every day. It was a bit of a chore making the trip from my house to Church, then back home for breakfast and back to school. It was difficult but I did it because I wanted to attend Mass daily. If you had asked me then to give an explanation "why," I would not have been able to give many reasons for it. There just was deep within me an almost irresistable attraction to Mass.

Since then I have reflected upon that youthful practice and have begun to understand more clearly what was going on.

How often the Lord works that way. Something happens, an attraction, an experience, a top of the mountain moment, whatever. Then we need some time to understand what the Lord has been doing. Only later do we exclaim: "Oh, that's what he's been trying to tell me." What a welcome, healing and loving experience it is when we finally see how God has been moving so powerfully in our lives.

As I said, I was drawn to the Mass when I was in the 7th and 8th grades. I'm a mixed breed - both public and parochial schools; but I was in a parochial school at that time. It had its consequences. My 8th grade teacher, Sister Irene Marie, told me, "Since you come to Mass every day you should become an altar boy." She added, "You probably know all about the Mass. Take this card home, and learn the Latin."

What an awful assignment that was! I may have the gift of tongues now, but that certainly did not include Latin and never in the 8th grade. I tried to learn the Latin as best I could. Besides, Sister said there would be a veteran altar boy at my first Mass as a shepherd to guide me. What a relief that was!

On the big day, my second debut in the Church (Baptism had not been my finest hour!), I got there and discovered that I would be serving the pastor. He was a most formidable man who liked me very much. (I didn't realize that at that particular time, however.) The pastor showed up, all the sisters showed up, the people showed up, and I showed up. Guess who never made an appearance? You're right. The veteran altar boy was nowhere to be found.

And so Mass began. One of the sisters came into the sacristy and rang the bells to take a little of the pressure off, and we finished the Mass. It was valid, I was assured. But, for me, the celebration was a bit of an agony. Nonetheless it was another and an important step on my way to the priesthood. I grew to love the Eucharist even more each time I was privileged to serve.

Two Opportunities

Bishop Sheen talked about two altar boys serving Mass. One of them did something stupid and the priest turned around and said, "Get out of here and never come back." That young boy never did come back. His name was Tito, the great leader of Yugoslavia; and what a loss he was to the Church.

The other altar boy lived in Peoria and one day served Mass for the Bishop in the cathedral. The poor kid dropped a cruet of wine. Sheen remarked that there is nothing comparable short of an atomic explosion to the sound of a crystal cruet shattering against a marble floor. The Bishop helped clean up and then finished the Mass. Afterward he said, "Did you ever think about becoming a priest?" And the boy said, "Yes." "Then I think you shall be a priest and go to Louvain someday for your studies." The boy went home and talked to his mother who told him that Louvain was the Catholic University of Belgium. Later on John Fulton Sheen did study for the priesthood at Louvain and became Bishop (eventually Archbishop) Fulton J. Sheen.

So , you see, God was reaching out to touch both boys at the Eucharist. One priest got in the way and messed up God's call; the other focused lovingly and com-passionately on who was serving his Mass, not the somewhat dramatic accident which happened.

God's ways are not our ways, but this we do know. The Lord is working to draw us to himself each moment of every day and no-

8

where more forcefully than at Eucharist.

Please, stop now in your reading, stretch a little and then do the following exercise. Take some time to think about two special Masses of your life:

the best and most satisfying one
and
the worst and most lifeless one.

Use the next two pages to describe each celebration. Try to remember the occasion or reason, the celebrant, congregation, and setting. Write your reflections on what your feelings and reactions were in this book. Let your creative literary juices flow. Take your time. Don't strain, but put some effort into it. You'll be doubly blessed.

Summary

After you have finished the exercises, please read this summary.

The Eucharist is the healing sacrament par excellence. When we gather to celebrate Eucharist we are entering into a deep and personal union with Jesus Christ. He comes to us in the Scriptures, in our prayers of praise and petition, and in his body and blood as they are shared with all who approach the table of sacrifice. When we gather together for Eucharist, love, health, and strength freely flow from Jesus to and through us because we are one with the source of all love and joy, of all health and goodness, of the strength we so sorely need but can never find within ourselves.

Now go back and reread your comments on the best and most satisfying Mass you ever participated in. Did it do what we just described? It came mighty close, I bet. Let's keep those memories and ideas firmly in mind as we move on to the next chapter.

CHAPTER TWO

A THEOLOGY OF THE EUCHARIST

As we begin I would like to present a brief theology of the Eucharist - not on a graduate level, but hopefully in the language that will be clear to most people. Some theologians use such esoteric language that few, if any, understand what they are saying. It is said that Father Karl Rahner's own brother (a most distinguished Jesuit scholar himself) once remarked that he could hardly understand what his brother was writing. Let's hope we can be clearer and speak with reverence and simplicity.

The Eucharist is explained in several words or phrases which have been helpful to me because most of them are traditional in our church. If I am quoting from some author, I will give proper credit. But unfortunately there may be times when I have so integrated the material that I am no longer aware of its authorship. God bless those authors and their great work in the church and, more to the point if they read this, may they be honored and forgive my completely unintentional transgression.

13

Words For The Eucharist

These are the words that help me to understand and fathom the theology of the Eucharist.

SACRAMENT

SACRIFICE

MEMORIAL

BANQUET

PRESENCE

PLEDGE OF ETERNAL GLORY

These six words /phrases are for me the basis upon which I build understanding of this tremendous mystery of God's love for us in Christ Jesus.

Sacrament

The Eucharist is a <u>sacrament</u>, one of the seven, but the greatest of the seven. It is not only an outward sign by which Jesus comes into intimate personal contact with us, but he is himself the sign. In it as sign is the living and breathing flesh and blood, body and mind, soul and divinity - the total being of the Lord Jesus Christ. In this sacrament the Lord seeks communion (union with) each one of us, his people. By

14

it we enter into communion with him, with ourselves and with all our other brothers and sisters, known and unknown, who make up his mystical body, the church.

Sacrifice

The Eucharist is the <u>sacrifice</u> which in an unbloody way re-enacts what Christ did on Calvary. He died after excruciating pain and suffering so that we might live in the freedom of God's children. He rescued us from sin and evil and gave us back our rightful inheritance. His sacrifice of himself fulfills and outshines all the sacrifices that ever were. No animal or mere human sacrifice could ever come near to the total emptying of himself which Jesus experienced on Calvary.

All peoples and all nations have offered sacrifices to their gods. In fact, they have regarded sacrifice as the supreme act of religion. At a certain point in history, however, God foretold a new, universal sacrifice, the sacrifice of his Son.

"I have no pleasure in you, says the Lord of Hosts;
neither will I accept any sacrifice from your hands,
For from the rising of the sun, even to its setting,
my name is great among the nations;
And everywhere they bring sacrifice to

my name,
     and a pure offering;
     For   great   is   my   name   among   the
nations,
     Says the Lord of Hosts." (Mal 1:10-11)

     In the Eucharist we renew the passion,
death, and resurrection of Jesus on our
altars around the world. As Paul wrote to
the Hebrews (9:13-14):

     "For if the blood of goats and bulls
and the sprinkling of a heifer's ashes can
sanctify those who are defiled so that
their flesh is cleansed, how much more will
the blood of Christ, who through the eternal spirit offers himself up unblemished to
God, cleanse our consciences from dead
works to worship the living God!"

                    A Memorial

     When we do the sacred action of the
Eucharist and participate in it as fully as
possible, we recall the death of the Lord
until he comes again. "Do this in memory of
me," he commands us. "Remember at this
<u>memorial</u> service what I have done for you,
what I have suffered for you. I have called
you out of exile, death, and sin into freedom, into a new life, my way of living."

     In 12-step programs, members are urged
to keep the "memories green," which means
never forget how bad it was before you hit

                         16

bottom. Let's keep our Eucharistic memories green also, and remember who was at the Last Supper and at Calvary. Get to know them and ask them to help you live this memorial of our faith with fresh insights and enthusiasm each time we "do this in remembrance" of the Lord.

Banquet

Eucharist is a <u>banquet</u>. Oftentimes we call it a memorial banquet in which we recall in a most vivid way the Last Supper. It is a banquet at which the Lord shares himself as our food and nourishment. "Take and eat. This is my body." "Take and drink. This is my blood given up for you. Do this in remembrance of me."

When the early Christians gathered they had a community meal at which they re-enacted what the Lord had done. But, as so often happens with human nature, some people began to abuse the meal aspects. Thus it came about that the Eucharistic service was separated from the agape meal. That may have been necessary but it has, I think, hindered our understanding of the community aspect of the shared meal, a special quality of every Eucharist.

Occasionally we celebrate a Christian Seder on some evening of Holy Week. A group gathers for the Seder meal doing exactly what the Lord Jesus did at the last supper.

After that ritual has been carried out
according to the Jewish tradition, Mass is
celebrated. It makes for rather a long but
fascinating and interesting evening. Some
prudent limitations on dessert and how long
it is enjoyed, plus some songs and prayers
of preparation and the Mass can begin in an
atmosphere of love and good family feelings. In a spirit of joy we reach back to
that Passover Meal Jesus celebrated with
his disciples - the first Christian Seder.
But the main benefit for me of having participated in the Christian Seder is that it
renews my sense of being rooted and ground-
ed in a banquet, a meal, in a ritual
memorial meal which is of vast historical
importance.

Presence

The Eucharist is a presence, but no
ordinary one. Rather it is that of the Lord
Jesus Christ. At Eucharist the Word in
Scripture is broken and shared with the
congregation. The Word of his body and
blood is broken and distributed at Communion. We in the Catholic Church reserve the
Eucharist under the species of consecrated
bread in the tabernacle. We believe the
Lord is truly present there. It is that
special presence which leads us to show
certain signs of respect such as tipping of
the hat, bowing of the head, or making the
sign of the cross, or one or more short
prayers.

How beautiful a custom it is to pray each time we pass a church.

"May the heart of Jesus in the Most Blessed Sacrament be praised, adored, and loved with grateful affection at every moment in all the tabernacles of the world even until the end of time."

If you know that prayer, continue to use it or begin to use it as you pass a church. If you do not know it, <u>take the time to write it out in the space below</u>. Make it your own, commit it to memory, and honor thereby the Lord, present in all the tabernacles of the world.

In the Northeastern section of the U.S., we are blessed with an abundance of churches and so have many opportunities to pay our loving respects to the Lord in the Blessed Sacrament. Try to be aware of each Church or chapel you pass, and pray to the Lord of the Eucharist for your needs of that moment or day.

Pledge of Eternal Glory

Each time we celebrate the Eucharist we receive the Lord of life, death, and resurrection. He has passed through the veil which separates us in this world from the next. He, our head, is <u>already</u> there and in that aspect or dimension we are also, but <u>not</u> <u>yet</u> fully there. However, what a great consolation in pain and suffering to be united with our Loving Savior who reigns in heavenly glory. Where he has gone, we are called to follow. We are with him, and in him, and through him we too will one day arrive home on that far distant shore which is our often longed-for and desired haven of peace and joy.

Remind yourself and others of this last dimension of the Eucharist. It has great power to energize and heal our doubts and fears about where we're going. We're going home and we are going to and with the one and only God-Man, Jesus the Lord.

A Personal Sharing

It is my firm conviction that the Catholic Church is on the verge of a great rebirth of devotion to the Eucharist. We're coming to a deeper understanding of the Eucharist in all of its dimensions. Our people are hungry. They have sought manna or Mannon in many places, but have not been satisfied. One woman who was raised a Catholic and who raised her family Catholic left the church in disgust and went to other churches. But she always came back. And it was the Eucharist which continually drew her back home.

One M.D. went out to investigate Oral Roberts' "City of Faith" hospital with an eye toward joining the staff. He loved the camaraderie with other Christian doctors, the freedom to pray and the ability to speak freely of his faith. However, there was no Eucharist and he felt that he could not live without it. At home he participated at Mass each day and found nourishment there which energized his whole day and ministry and practice. He could never see himself without the Eucharist each day.

Others feel the same way and still others are coming to such a realization. There is a great revival coming. The signs are clear. Be a part of it. In fact, help to make it happen. Lead the way by inviting others to come with you. Not only invite them, but offer to take them to church. Help the process get moving in your area. Jump on the bandwagon if it's already begun. <u>Be</u> <u>a</u> <u>part</u> <u>of</u> <u>the</u> <u>victory</u>.

The Lord is going to save his body. Times look dark and dangerous; the waters in which we sail are threatening and wild; but guess who is still in charge? The Lord, and he is about to bring forth from all the turmoil and difficulty a new and greater sense of community and faithfulness and love.

CHAPTER THREE

SACRAMENTAL SYSTEMS

"Sacramental systems." The combination of these words hangs in the air before me and suddenly a myriad of ideas, images, and memories swirl around that phrase, forming in my mind a question, like Joseph's coat, of many colors.

As pre-Vatican II children we were taught that a sacrament was "an outward sign instituted by Christ to give grace." In some way we may have visualized a type of "God is a faucet" theology, turning grace on and off whenever we received a sacrament and keeping it open for however long it lasted and then shutting it off when we were finished. Then along came Vatican II and suddenly God was explained to us no longer as a grace-dispensing faucet but as an unending and unquenchable torrent of grace, love, and healing. Sacraments became "encounters with God." All well and good. Wonderful, in fact!

However, since my experience of encounters with the Almighty is anything but systematic, I am at once perplexed and enthralled, repelled and yet strongly attracted, by that phrase. I suppose that's the cause of my multi-colored reaction and question: how can there be a thing called a "sacramental system"?

I am so struck with that word "system." My life, all our lives are filled with systems. Indeed, the yellow pages give written witness to the systems of systems that control our temporal destinies. We even do systems analysis (systematically, of course) to discover what in our systems does or doesn't work well. Until recently most of our systems sought to maximize corporate profits or industrial production. Only lately(and many would say belatedly) do our systems seek to maximize human potential.

Our systems - governmental, social, economic - are usually designed for <u>efficiency</u>. God's systems are designed for <u>efficacy</u>, and thank God for that grace. However, let's use systems' language and framework to gain the greatest benefit we can.

People embrace systems because they work . . . or the people believe they work, which is almost as good. From picking a horse to organizing a kitchen to arranging a set of files, everyone has a system. And each of those systems depends on some basic core or premise to make it work.

Well, it would appear we have created

our human systems in that one respect at least on God's model; even if we have fallen woefully short of his built-in regard for the life of the universe. Because our sacramental system has a core as well, a sacred heartbeat that brings order to the system and life to those of us who use it. That <u>core</u> <u>is</u> <u>Jesus</u> <u>Christ</u>.

Basically the system may be bent – though never broken – into three main areas: sacraments of initiation, sacraments of growth and community, and sacraments of healing. While each area contains differing facets, one facet remains constant throughout the system. That <u>facet</u> <u>is</u> <u>Jesus</u> <u>Christ</u>.

We can see too that the system is designed to nourish us in each of our life passages: Baptism, Confirmation, Matrimony, Holy Orders, Anointing of the Sick, Reconciliation, and <u>Eucharist</u> and <u>Eucharist</u> and <u>Eucharist</u>. That's no "typo," but shows us that Eucharist falls into all three categories: initiation, growth, and healing. None of these exists outside of or without the real, tangible presence of Christ in the Eucharist. When the emphasis is so great, so constant, we must acknowledge the nourishment which most deeply pervades the system. That <u>nourishment</u> <u>is</u> <u>Jesus</u> <u>Christ</u>.

What/who calls us into being, urges us to growth, feeds and heals us more than the "love of God poured out in Christ Jesus"? And what greater way does Christ come to us than in the blinding rapturous moment of Communion, union-with?

To call this a "system" is, I guess, symptomatic of much of our God-language and indicative of our human condition. We need to create some order, some method of quantifying what would otherwise bring us to our knees gasping at such ineffable greatness, such profusion of the inexplicable.

And so, we speak of a "system" for the sacraments. It is good for it gives us a vocabulary. It is good for it reminds us of the importance of our life passages and keeps them within the perspective of God. And it is good because it never fails to acknowledge the necessity and centrality of Jesus Christ.

In some seminary class or other I remember hearing the phrase "the diaphony of Christ" (his transparent presence like a veil through which everything is seen). Those are such beautiful words, presenting such a wonderful world view. And, it seems to me, that they describe in a burst of poetry our sacramental system, which exists through, with and in this Christological diaphony.

We do not see, except through Christ. Our vision of the Father comes only through what we see of the Son. Nor, I believe, does our Father see us except through

26

Christ. He is the point at which heaven and earth meet, mix, speak, even perhaps make love.

Eucharist is our most intimate moment. And I mean that without reservation. There is no other act in which two can literally become one. More than one flesh. More than one spirit. In Eucharist we are united with Jesus Christ, God, Lord of the Universe, in a sacred union that, quite honestly, is beyond my understanding or ability to express adequately. And yet the effort to do so by you and me, as we are doing now, does us great honor.

It is enough for you and me that all the above is true, and it is.

It is more than enough for you and me that he is.

Understanding The System

In my teaching career at Caldwell College I used several examples or designs to explain the sacraments. They seemed to be helpful to the students.

First we considered the sacramental system as a wheel. This will be apparent if you try to visualize the sacraments as a wheel with the hub being the Eucharist. Out of it flow the other sacraments: Baptism and Confirmation, Penance and Holy Orders and Matrimony and the Anointing of the Sick. As a result of the reforms of Vatican II, the Church now celebrates many of the sacraments within a Eucharistic setting. This highlights what we are saying.

Baptism may be celebrated in the Eucharist. Confirmation most often is. Holy Orders always has been and Matrimony often is at a nuptial Mass. The Anointing of the Sick may also be. Have you ever been at a communal Anointing of the Sick? It's a very beautiful service. The only sacrament not celebrated at the Eucharist is Penance or Reconciliation.

No matter whether you or a loved one receives a sacrament at Mass, try to see the connection. Better yet, remind yourself and others of this fact. The Church often encourages couples and families who are not having their marriages or baptisms at Mass to attend the Eucharist earlier in the day. Keep the connection strong and vivid. Believe and proclaim it. Encourage relatives and friends to participate in the Eucharist before such occasions. Evangelize them in this way.

A Three-Fold Image

Another way to understand the sacramental system is threefold: Initiation, Growth and Healing.

In my religious education classes at Caldwell, I would diagram this concept as follows:

Sacraments of Initiation
Baptism, Confirmation, Eucharist

Sacraments of Healing
Anointing of the Sick, Penance-Reconciliation, Eucharist

Sacraments of Growth
Holy Orders, Matrimony, Eucharist

Usually I would then ask the students how many sacraments there were. One of them would always answer, "nine," at which time I would point out that we are still maintaining that there are seven sacraments which the Lord gave us. The Eucharist is in all three categories because the Lord Jesus Christ is involved in all of these phases of our lives as his followers.

Sacraments of Initiation

Sacraments of Initiation celebrate and effect the beginnings of our life of faith, our journey with the Lord. The Churches of the Eastern Rite (some are in union with the Pope) give the sacraments of initiation to the infant all at one time. In our tradition that's not the case as we seek to educate and train the child in its faith life. In the Rite of Christian Initiation of Adults, the catechumen receives the three sacraments of Initiation at the Easter Vigil Service.

Too often Initiation is limited (at least in our emphases) to our First Holy Communion. Now granted that the time of First Holy Communion is a tremendously important one, I think it still has to be acknowledged that for most people it is a symbolically significant rite of passage, although hopefully no first communicant will have the vaguest idea what that means.

One religious sister remarked that her First Communion excitement was confined to having a beautiful dress to wear and being the center of attention. As to the Eucharist itself, Sister says, "I just remember thinking that the host tasted like cardboard."

"Sister says" has great power for us. "Sister says" is a phrase that has been used to open more doors and get more of the church moving than almost any other phrase I know. Sister says, "Don't you dare chew the host," and we almost gag trying to swallow it untouched. What Sister has just said about her first Holy Communion is quite typical for girls. As a young boy I can remember a blue suit, a new watch, and hurrying to my grandparents with great expectations of some wonderful cake and a few more dollars to add to my kitty.

I don't feel particularly guilty about those memories, and I don't think Sister does either, because the Lord was involved in the whole experience. The Lord was stressing the gift of himself; and these other, less significant gifts had their place. Family celebrations and parties and food which was shared also spoke mightily to some of the eternal verities which make us a community of faith. You know, perhaps it was our narrow view of what Communion meant which prevented us from accepting all of these things as part of the celebration.

St. Therese of Lisieux speaks about her First Communion in a way that I admire and which I hope would be reality for me by the time I reach my _last_ Holy Communion. But I don't intend to beat myself over the head or shoulders or any other part of my anatomy in guilt because I did not have a similar experience.

The other great consolation is that initiation is not a once-in-a-lifetime thing but is an ongoing process through all of our formative years and even beyond. I think of Eucharist as a sacrament of initiation into the various and continuing stages of our Christian life journey.

Sacraments of Growth

The Sacraments of Growth build community. They are body-building events in our faith journey, building up the body of Christ by making Christians stronger and truer to their calling.

We grow day by day and usually because we're eating three square meals a day. A friend of mine has coffee for breakfast with a piece of protein bread, a little fruit and perhaps a cracker for lunch, and then a big - sometimes huge - meal in the evening, most often Italian. That's one way to be nourished.

Another way says that we are to eat like kings at breakfast, princes at lunch, and paupers at supper/dinner. Far be it from me to make a play on words, but eating like a king at breakfast or in the morning has always reminded me of the Eucharist. Daily Mass so often takes place in the morning and it is a kingly meal. As we will say in another place in this book, it's the best meal I ever had.

Sacraments of Healing

Healing is involved in every sacrament but three sacraments most highlight this element. Penance - Reconciliation, the Anointing of the Sick, and the Eucharist bring Christians to greater health in body, mind, and spirit. Too often they seem in- effective because we Catholics do not ex- pect much to happen, and so very little does. In Nazareth Jesus could work few

miracles (healings) because of the towns-
people's lack of faith. The same is true
today. Our faith needs to be stirred.

Eucharist as a sacrament of healing to
me means that the Lord is renewing himself
in us. We are renewing ourselves in him is
another way to put it. There is great power
for renewal in this sacrament.

Secondly, this is the sacrament by and
in which Jesus is repairing our hurts and
wounds, the gaps between the love we needed
and the love we received, the potholes of
life which unfortunately bedevil our
journey. We may not often think about the
Lord as a repairman, but I don't know why
we don't. There's no reason not to. He was
a carpenter, wasn't he?

He is, in one image, the garbageman
par excellence because he's asking us to
surrender the garbage of our lives, not
just the garbage of sin but also the
garbage of guilt, resentment, hatred, fear,
and other emotions which are not always
sinful but can be quite harmful.

Finally, in the Eucharist I see the
Lord healing our self-image. He is helping
us to realize in a deeper way who we really
are and whose we really are.

Healing of our self-image is something
we are in desperate need of in these times.
Sister Ruthann Williams, O.P., from our In-

stitute staff, has done several days on the healing of women. They have been very, very well attended and received which speaks volumes about the need for these kinds of days. Sister uses scriptural women to illustrate God's delight in the feminine, creation's need for both masculine and feminine, and Jesus' call to greater freedom for all people. There has been healing in this discovery for many women. I hope to be able, using masculine models, to do the same for men.

One priest remarked about how beautiful their parish's communal celebration of the Anointing of the Sick had been. Those who participated were delighted with the service which is quite personal and affirming, and they loved the refreshments and sharing of community afterward. "Of course," the priest added, "no one was healed." That's negativity in spades! No one may have thrown aside a walker, cane or crutch, but our faith tells us that Jesus Christ really did touch each person. Perhaps we priests and all participants have to spend some time renewing and revitalizing our faith in the Lord's power.

Too often we presume that because people are there for the service, they obviously believe. That is true to some extent, but I know it's not enough. They and we priests also need a good faith jump start to get us believing and moving on all cells. There's a power of positive believing at work here which is as powerful as our ability to believe. And that's pretty powerful!

However all that may be, notice that the Eucharist is in each of the three categories. The centrality and importance of the Eucharist is clear. Why not think about the Eucharist in these three main ways. It is the sacrament which helped you _in the beginning_ of your faith life. It is the sacrament that sustains you _in growth_, also it is the sacrament that _heals you_ in your relationships with God, neighbor, and self.

It is a source of holiness and wholeness. It is _Jesus Christ_, _our greatest healing gift_.

CHAPTER FOUR

THE GREATEST HEALING SERVICE

There are many aspects of the Eucharist which have great power in the healing process. At the Institute we arrange and celebrate Healing Masses. And not infrequently we are asked the question: What exactly is a Healing Mass? Some way out experimental, faddish liturgical experiment? By no means.

A Healing Mass is the Eucharistic celebration carried out exactly as the Church prescribes, but with a greater emphasis on its healing aspects. Usually there is more time for the celebration so that allows for longer periods of prayer, praise, and silence.

Let's examine what happens at a Healing Mass, and let our own perceptions of Eucharist be heightened so that we will be able to participate in any Eucharistic celebration with a more powerful knowledge of God's healing love.

Please, remember that every Eucharistic celebration is a healing service in which we celebrate God's love for us. In it

we give thanks to the Father through Jesus,
our great and high priest, in the power of
the Holy Spirit, who makes us a community
of believers and receivers.

The Liturgy Of The Word

At the Penitential Rite we ask Jesus
to take all the garbage of sinful attitudes
and actions out of our lives. We acknowledge our sins, express our sorrow, and
then give those sins away to Jesus. In
faith and trust we let go of them and of
guilt and shame.

We listen to the Word of God contained
in the readings and the homily. And we seek
to take that Word into our daily lives,
make it a part of us and all we experience,
listening with special care for the Special
Word God has for us at that moment. We
treasure that word, taking it into our
hearts, minds, and wills.

At the Prayer of the Faithful we mention many people and causes. We also remember those who are ill and also those who
care for them, especially medical and
health-care professionals.

Gifts and Eucharistic Prayer

During the Offertory procession, we
present ourselves to God for his service

and love, even as we offer our gifts of bread and wine.

At the Consecration we are in awe of God's power as our gifts of bread and wine become the body and blood of Christ. As our acclamation we often use: "Lord, by your cross and resurrection you have set us free. You are the Savior of the world." We claim the freedom from fear, death, sin and evil which Christ has won for us.

The Family Prayer

The Our Father provides us with an opportunity to stand in the truth that we are beloved children of God our Father. We may at times spontaneously join hands to signify that we belong to the family of God. Before praying for peace and exchanging a greeting of peace, we ask the Lord to help us forgive those who have hurt or wounded us. Jesus, who forgave those who executed him, invites us to let go of resentment, grudges, and jealousy. He not only invites but gives us the grace that enables us to do so.

Communion and After

As we receive the Lord at Communion we express our belief in his presence by saying, "Amen." Then we silently continue, "I believe, Lord, that you are healing me of

39

my (mention the physical or emotional ail-
ment)." This is a time to stir up the
embers of our faith into living flames. We
preach to ourselves about the real presence
of Jesus in our total being and try to act
accordingly.

After Communion we usually have a time
of complete silence for five or ten minutes
when we let Jesus love us into a new and
more vital life in whatever way he wants.
It isn't easy for us to get quiet to the
degree in which healing can take place.
But, please, try to calm and focus
yourself. The time after Communion is a
graced moment and very often there is a
simply beautiful peace and contentment
which comes over us.

Blessing The Lord's People

At the conclusion of the Mass the
priests and/or deacons usually bless each
person and lay hands on them. The personal
touch is so important because each of us
wants special attention and wants to feel
personally affirmed and loved. Too often we
experience the opposite.

What's your social security number or
may I see your credit card? Even when a
person has the cash in hand, no car rental
agency, that I know of, will give him or
her a car without a major credit card for
reference, security, or whatever.

40

In such a world how important it is to be touched personally and lovingly by the Lord through his healing priests and people.

Often we use blessed oil, one of the church's sacramentals, like holy water, and say a short prayer for the individual. This is not usually the Sacrament of the Anointing of the Sick. If you wish to receive that healing sacrament, just mention it to the priest.

Afterward persons may choose to go to a team of two or more people who will pray with them for any special needs. This is body ministry - whereby members of Christ's body who have some experience in these matters - pray as a healing team and ask Jesus to anoint and use their words and gestures.

Please, don't ever forget however, the utterly essential fact that the Eucharist by itself is enough. All the rest is just an attempt to highlight, underline, and emphasize what Jesus has already done in the Eucharist.

The few short paragraphs above are the briefest explanation of what we mean by a Healing Mass. You really need to experience such a Mass, not just read about it.

Thank God many priests are celebrating the Eucharist this way or in similar ways

today. Please go to a healing Mass, and
please suspend all your doubts and
questions! Enter as fully as you can into
this experience of worship, praise and
adoration. In fact, why nct come prepared
by some quiet time and with a deep hunger
for healing? The Lord really finds it hard
to resist such faith and longing. Just read
the Gospels, especially Mark and Luke.

A Healing Time or
A Time For Healing

One of the special moments at a Healing Mass comes after Communion when we
often ask the people to be absolutely quiet
for five or ten minutes while they just
rest in the healing love of Jesus. The
first time I suggested this extended period
of quiet, I wasn't certain how the congregation would respond. What followed was
truly amazing. A silence settled over the
group, a silence so profound and so
peaceful that I knew the Spirit was "a-
movin'" in great power. Only one person
hadn't calmed down and that was me. Then
the Lord suggested, "They're okay. Now,
what about you?" So I willingly and eagerly
yielded to his love so strongly manifested
in that silence which was so deep and healing, so filled with his special love.

Normally as I indicated it takes me
quite a while just to settle down. I begin
by making an act of faith in the presence

of Jesus , God and human, dwelling in me. Recently while doing that I was more distracted than normal by various things that were going on. But the words I kept hearing and the sentiments within my heart were "Trust me; you can rely on me." At the conclusion of our silent time with the Lord, which had been very good, if just a bit distracting, I opened the Missal and read these words in the Communion antiphon, "You can rely on me. You can always depend upon me to be your strength. I have given you freedom." They were a paraphrase of Psalm 18, verse 3. "You, Lord, are my rock, my refuge, my fortress, my God in whom I trust."

These words reminded me of the power of the Lord to meet and address my particular needs. The Lord often does speak that clearly in such deep, silent healing moments. Oftentimes he is much more muted, but at that particular time in my life, he clearly spoke to the point. It was a reaffirmation of my conviction, "I can trust the Lord. I can rely on him."

Some Words Of Caution

At healing Masses some people wait impatiently for the end of Mass so they can be blessed. They can hardly wait for Mass to be over because they confusedly think that the individual blessing is the important time. I <u>hate</u> that attitude and try my best to _blast_ it out of people's minds. The force of those words "hate" and "blast" points out how serious a deception and confusion that approach is. What a perversion of reality to mistake the minister for the Lord Jesus Christ.

On the other hand, don't be of the mentality that says Jesus heals only at Eucharist, or at a special gathering of your prayer group, or at a large healing service or whatever. The fact is that Jesus is healing now, while you - wherever you are - read these words and seek to apply them.

Jesus Is Healing Now

Please, open your eyes and do not miss what the Lord is doing now. Don't be so caught up in waiting for the magic moment for healing that you miss the very ordinary moment when the Lord wants to touch you with his healing power. Jesus did not wait for magic moments to heal someone. He normally waited for only one thing - a person's heart to be open to God's grace.

Yes! Yes! Yes!

When we advertise that we're having a Healing Mass at a certain parish, someone will remark, "Isn't every Mass a Healing Mass?" I readily agree, but unfortunately

44

many people think that's not the case unless one of the priests involved in the healing ministry is the celebrant, or some other equally arbitrary quality is present.

<u>EVERY</u> <u>MASS</u> <u>IS</u> <u>A</u> <u>HEALING</u> <u>SERVICE</u> <u>OF</u> <u>THE</u> <u>WORD</u> <u>OF</u> <u>GOD</u>: <u>JESUS</u> <u>CHRIST</u>, broken and distributed for us in the Scriptural readings and in Communion. Both of these parts are united and vivified by the Eucharistic prayer in which the bread and wine are consecrated into the Body and Blood of Christ.

Label It

People love to put labels on others. When I celebrated my 25th anniversary of ordination, our Archdiocesan newspaper headlined the story: "Healing Priest Celebrates 25th." Another priest who is a multi-talented individual usually gets the label "Motorcycle Priest" because he rides a humongous motorcycle, organized the Catholic Motorcycle Club of New Jersey, and has a special ceremony each year at which he blesses the club members and their bikes. Then he celebrates MASS with them (and he also hears confessions). Wow! do they participate because Father Mark is there and so are three hundred or more of their brothers and sisters from the club. He really works at this ministry as he does the other one hundred or so ministries he's juggling.

If we have to put labels on things, let's get the right label for the Eucharist. It's the <u>Healing</u> <u>Service</u> <u>par</u> <u>excellence</u>.

The Lord's Cry

And the Lord is saying, "Come, come and be with me. Let me touch you and heal you." All of us have daily hurts and the Lord at the daily Eucharist wants to heal us of those hurts, wants to give us those few moments really to experience his love.

Do yourself a favor and think about every Mass as a Healing Mass. Be very positive and convincing to yourself and others. Start saying, "I'm going to a healing service where the Lord will touch me, calm me, heal me, and love me, where he'll change hearts, mine and others." Father Bertolucci with great power and enthusiasm has proclaimed that your presence and attitude at the Eucharist makes a tremendous difference.

The Priest

If the priest seems discouraged and out of sorts, pray for him, intercede for him, and love and affirm him.

Having just finished an almost two-year stint as pastor of a large suburban parish, and after twenty-nine+ years of priesthood, I can testify to the pressures on priests today. These are multitudinous. Our own parents or siblings may be ill, handicapped, or otherwise severely restricted. We may be experiencing personal health problems, personality problems among the staff, etc., etc. And then taking supervisory care of the whole physical plant. Add to all these the continued pressure to be all things to all men and women plus the need to grow emotionally and integrate so much into our own lives. Believe me, there are pressures on a priest today that are far different and, I believe, far more exhausting and forbidding than years ago. Like the rest of humans (and remember, we are very human) we have different personalities and styles of relating. We are at vastly different stages of growth and emotional development.

Some Suggestions

Why not tell your priest of your love, affection, and continuing prayer for him each day? He may faint, but he'll love it. However, pray for the guidance and wisdom from God to know when and where to speak or write to him. Many times a combination of both is the better - a gentle word of encouragement, followed by a cheerful card (it's easier for you to write and for him to read) with a few more words of encouragement.

How Are You Feeling?

If you're not feeling up to par, pray for yourself, be gentle and loving with yourself also. Turn off some of the noise and clatter of your world. Concentrate on the Lord and his word spoken or whispered to you. Take an "instant vacation" with him by closing your eyes and shutting down your hyperactive mood and breathing deeply but gently. Then you may want to whisper your own serenity prayer or the one used at 12-step meetings:

God, grant me the <u>Serenity</u> to accept the things I cannot change,
<u>Courage</u> to change the things I can, and
<u>Wisdom</u> to know the difference.

A Final Note

Just a final note regarding "Healing Masses." Try to adapt what we have said. Apply what you learned and experienced to each and every Eucharistic celebration you attend. Jesus truly comes into intimate personal contact with us in every sacrament but no where more than in the Eucharist. Celebrate it always, or as often as you can, as the healing service par excellence. Make a good effort at this and when you can "do your best." Otherwise, make whatever effort you can: good, moderate, weak, or poor. It will be enough for that moment.

CHAPTER FIVE

OUR EUCHARISTIC COMPANION

In the Eucharist the Lord wants to touch us. He heals us, and he does so in the best and worst times we experience. What he said to his disciples, he says to us. For you, it is impossible, "but for God all things are possible." (Matthew 19:26)

We believe that Jesus is the Son of God who made heaven and earth; things visible and invisible. We believe in him as a God of love and power who is with us in good times and in bad, in sunshine and rain, no matter how dark the hour may seem or how much pain we may have to bear. As Jesus hung on the cross he suffered agonies which we will never understand. He was the most sensitive human being who ever lived, so he suffered even more than we can ever imagine. He did not do it because he enjoyed suffering. He did it because he wanted to be the perfect and special companion of his people in good times and in bad, in times of radiant glowing health as well as in times of pain and racking illness.

In the Eucharist Jesus is with us in a

49

special way to companion us on our journey home. He is definitely with us in many other ways, but in the Eucharist he is there unmistakably and completely.

Skin Hunger

Someone told me recently that there is in every human being a phenomenon called "skin hunger," hunger for the touch of another human being. Notice how most humans have a strong urge to hold a baby, and notice how the infant responds and wants to be held and loved, played with and spoken to, even in the gibberish we call "baby talk." It is a sign of abnormality when an infant does not want to be held or even resists loving attention.

I'm An S.O.G.

I have two grandchildren (which is quite a good move for a celibate). I "adopted" their parents so I could be an "S.O.G." (Silly Old Grandparent)

How Mary Ellen Clare and C.J. (Clinton Joseph) love to be held! I've even held C.J. during my homily. We make quite a team. He gurgles and looks adorable while I preach about the love of God. His noises and movements (at least at six months) are never distracting, but rather a real asset because he's being, acting, and proclaiming that he is God's beloved child. He has no need to explain why he's at the lectern during the Eucharistic homily. He belongs, is loved, and loves it. He truly is the King's kid.

My Prayer For Them And All Of Us

May C.J. and Mary Ellen Clare always know love in its many facets. And may each one of us move in the same freedom and knowledge.

In the Eucharist Jesus comes to love us and he does not hold back. He gives himself to us completely to fulfill our "skin hunger" and the other hungers buried deep within our hearts. We are his Mary Ellen Clares and C.J.'s and much more.

Assurance and More

People who seek prayers for inner healing need to be assured of the love of the Lord which will take the place of the love they never received from one or both parents. Parents, at times, and especially some fathers, seem to think that all they have to do is to provide clothing, food and shelter for their children.

In volume one of "The Healing Journey" series, there is a story of a priest whose father had never held him or said, "I love you." Deep within, the son - now an adult - felt a tremendous gap and was endlessly longing for the assurance that he was loveable. At least the orphan within him was longing for it.

Intellectually he had all the answers, but emotionally he was a cripple. Even the prayer for inner healing he had received was not enough to touch, ease, and heal the emotional hurt which was terribly deep seated and engraved. He needed more! Once was definitely not enough.*

For such a person and for all of us in similar circumstances, Jesus is the answer. Jesus in the Eucharist provides us with his body and blood, his soul and his divinity - his complete self. He embraces us in a way that no one else can ever do. The intimacy of his presence to us in the Eucharist is almost too much for us to comprehend. But

---

*N.B. In similar cases I recommend a multi-faceted approach. My prescription is: 1) daily Mass and Communion; 2)a Holy Hour each day; 3) active participation in a 12-step group such as Emotions Anonymous, Adult Children of Alcoholics, Al-Anon, etc. 4) seeking out the best therapist possible and being faithful to your appointments. If you need a reference, contact me or the Association of Christian Therapists at 1-301-470-2287.

try your best to be open to it. Let his love envelop and calm you, touch and heal you.

Any Effort Will Be Rewarded

This dimension of the Eucharist is so important that it demands strenuous and deliberate efforts to penetrate as much as we can of this extraordinary gift of God's love. Think about your hunger for love and affection, and then bring it to the Lord in the Eucharist. No one is suggesting that Jesus will usurp the place of your loved ones. That is not the way he works. However he does remind you and me that he has always loved us, loves us now with an unlimited love, and will always love us with that same limitless love.

Claim for yourself all the graces which God offers to you. Ask the Lord to help you to understand the abundance of his love made present to you in every sacrament and, most especially, in the sacrament of the Eucharist. Stir up the graces of your Baptism and Confirmation and claim your inheritance as God's beloved child. Ask God to renew within you the grace of every sacrament you have received, and particularly every encounter with him in Eucharist.

Everyone Loves A Bride!

The Lord delights to be with his people and to share their good times and their bad times. Remember the bridal imagery which he used so often in the Scriptures. Picture a newly wed couple on their honeymoon. See how they look at each other, how they say things just by a glance or a touch, how they love to be close together. There's almost a fascination about discovering the other person in new and deeper ways. The Lord God wants to be our bridegroom and enter into that type of bridal relationship with each of us.

Believe it when the Lord says, "I take you to be my special one. I take you for better, for worse, for richer, for poorer, in sickness and in health, until death and beyond death, since death is no barrier to me. I have conquered death and I call you to share in my victory." In the Eucharist Jesus speaks words even more healing than those above. Listen to Jesus within you at such times.

The Best Meal I Ever Had

One of our religious sisters who spends her life visiting people in her parish tells the following story:

One day as she was canvassing a certain street, she met a young man. He was unshaven and obviously on his way to a gym. She introduced herself and told him of her work visiting the Catholics in the area. His reaction: "Sister, I'm no longer a Catholic. I've been excommunicated." Her "Oh, how did that happen?" elicited the following: "Well, I've been divorced so that's how I know I've been excommunicated." Her reply was brief and to the point: "Do you have the letter from the Bishop?" "Hell, no! (Oh, I'm sorry, Sister.) Why should he write to me?" "Then I don't think you can be excommunicated," Sister replied. Stuttering a little bit, the young man insisted that he was doubly excommunicated because he'd been divorced twice. She countered with "that means you have to have two letters from the Bishop."

The young man scratched his head and went on to talk about his two marriages. They had both been civil marriages and had each lasted just a short time. Sister reassured him that all he had to do was to go to confession. "And wasn't it grand that in the parish confessions were heard every day after the noon Mass?" He left her with the promise that he would certainly think about it.

Another "No Show"?

She kept an eye out for him at all that weekend's Masses but he didn't appear. In the middle of the week she received a

55

letter. He hadn't worked up the nerve to go on the weekend, but when Monday came, it brought a sure conviction that today had to be the day. He went to confession, the priest was wonderful, and so he received Communion. He concluded his letter with the words: "Sister, that was the best meal I ever had."

A postscript to this particular graced moment came when the Sister showed the letter to the pastor. He was so struck by it that he decided to quote it in his Sunday homily. Guess who was sitting at the pastor's Mass on Sunday? The young man was right there when the priest read the letter. In fact, the priest built his whole homily around the sentence: "Sister, that was the best meal I ever had."

Hey, Mom! Look!

The young man later told the Sister that he literally flew home and called his mother. She had been praying for years that he would come back to the Church. He was so enthusiastic that he shouted, "Mom, the priest preached about me at Mass today." Calming down, he then reassured her that it had been a positive experience. He told her the story and said that he was definitely back in the fold and going to receive the sacraments. In fact, he was determined to get to Mass as often as he possibly could.

The beautiful part of Sister's ministry, by the way, is that she is there each
day and especially at every weekend Mass.
She keeps a loving and affirming eye on her
people. She is truly a good shepherd!

Meditation

Think about the best meal that you
ever had. Was it Thanksgiving, Christmas,
Easter? Who was there and what made it so
special? I believe, and this is a personal
opinion, that the food is important but the
company is much more important for an en-
joyable meal.

In the Eucharist we have the utterly
unique situation of having both the best
meal and the best company, the Lord Jesus
Christ. We come to feast at the banquet of
the Lord, and he is our food and drink.

Why not translate "it was the best
meal I ever had" to "it is and always will
be the best meal"?

The Eucharistic banquet to which we
are invited with such prodigality by the
Lord is always the best meal we can ever
have. Rejoice and be glad that we are
called to celebrate with the Church and
participate in this most special banquet.

More than A Gala

As I finish this chapter, I am getting ready to attend a Gala banquet to support a cause close to my heart, St. Catherine's Infirmary in Caldwell. That's the residence where my mother has been lovingly cared for by the Dominican sisters since 1974 after her first stroke. Each ticket to the Gala is $100 and I'm sure it will be a good meal. But it will never compare to the Eucharistic banquet no matter how much care and effort go into it.

A Better Meal

Recently I shared a meal with friends. The cook had outdone herself and the food was exquisitely prepared and lovingly served. That type of meal is far better than any banquet in a restaurant, especially since she had made my favorite dessert: lemon meringue pie.

The Best

The Eucharist is a home-cooked lovingly prepared meal, and it is "the best meal" we can ever have.

Buon appetito!!!

CHAPTER SIX

EUCHARIST AND THE BODY OF CHRIST

One beautiful and meaningful image that Paul gives us is the image of the mystical body of Christ. Christ is the head and we all are members, cells in his Body. A contemporary painting shows the head and shoulders of Christ and they are filled with the profiles or busts of many famous and not so famous people.

It is another reminder that Christ is truly in his people and his people are in him. This teaching of St. Paul and of the Church about the mystical body of Christ is a great and consoling doctrine. May it help us to approach the Eucharistic table knowing we are never alone. We are always connected to and part of a very holy family.

A bumper sticker has the following message:
God is my Father
    Jesus is my Brother
        The Holy Spirit makes me his
          Temple
Mary is my Mother
        All the Saints and Angels are my
          relatives
        That's some family I've got!

Quite a message and it's all true. But do not make one and try to use it because it would take quite a bumper to hold it! Besides, I almost ran into the truck myself trying to read it.

This particular concept of the Body of Christ touched a young woman deeply. She realized that every time she tried to hurt or even the score with another individual, she was hurting herself because she was hurting the roots which fed her as well as the other person.

You're Hurting Me!

Jesus gave a similar revelation to Saul on his way to Damascus to persecute the early Christians, followers of the Way - Jesus. "Saul, Saul, why are you persecuting me?" Saul cried out, "Who are you?" And Jesus told him who he was - the Christ, the Nazarene. He was being hurt not in himself physically, but in his body the Church, the community of his followers. Jesus was truly being hurt by what Saul was doing in persecuting his faithful followers, the members of his mystical body. And it is still going on. When we hurt another human being, we hurt not only him or her, but ourselves and all humans, and also the Lord. That's the negative side of this great mystery of our interrelatedness in Jesus Christ.

There are tremendous positive effects when any Christian, any part of the body, is loving and serving the Lord, coming to know the Lord in a deeper way and trusting more fully in him. When one of us reaches out to help the sick, wounded, ill, a poor brother or sister, then the root system is getting stronger and the body is also. This is truly Christ's work and he calls us to himself, to share himself with us in the Eucharist and so form us into his body.

Accepting The Lord's Vision

"Look beyond the bread you eat, look beyond the cup you drink, see your Savior and your Lord" are beautiful words from a contemporary hymn. What a challenge for all of us to let go of our myopia and accept the Lord's vision. Let us see how much each individual human being is worth in the eyes of Christ. Then endeavor to treat that person accordingly.

Do this at the Eucharist by prayer and kindly looks and actions. Do it at the greeting of peace and before and after Mass. Please be aware of the brother or sister who is new to the congregation, not a stranger in your midst but just a friend you haven't met yet but are going to do so as soon as possible.

Faith's Vision

An evangelist, Faith Smith, once told a group of priests who were on retreat a vision the Lord had given her. She shared in true humility (no apologies for the gift she had been given, just a straightforward proclamation of who deserved the credit). She was praying in a Catholic church, but was not yet a member. At Communion as the people were approaching the priest to receive, she saw the Lord move into the body of the priest distributing Communion. She saw Jesus Christ the Lord sharing his own body and blood. All around the person receiving, Faith saw a multitude of angels and humans rejoicing with great joy at what was taking place.

She delighted in the revelation of what was happening in the spiritual realm, and asked the Lord what lessons he was trying to teach her. She was told by the Lord that all the people there were the deceased loved ones and relatives of the person receiving and that there were strong and vibrant bonds of love uniting all of them. They were not alone and would never, in fact, could never, receive Communion isolated and alone because that's a contradiction in terms (oxymoronic statement, if you will).

What a consoling thought and image. See if it speaks to you. It certainly did to me and I use it often when I'm receiving and when watching others receive.

Corpus Christi

I subscribed for many years to a family prayer and reflection service called "Together," published by Families for Prayer, 775 Madison Avenue, Albany, NY 12208. It was so good that I gave gift subscriptions to my three sisters and two brothers and many of my friends.

On the feast of Corpus Christi* it ran the reflection which follows. Please, read it carefully. In some limited ways it confirms what Faith Smith saw in her vision. It has helped me. Perhaps it will help you.

"What do you do when you return to your place after receiving Communion at Mass? Do you kneel and bury your head in your arms? Do you sit and allow peace to fill your heart? Do you join in singing the communion song or just listen to the music? Perhaps you read prayers of thanksgiving

---

*Corpus Christi is the feast at which we celebrate the reality of the Eucharist with almost unreserved joy and happiness. We cannot do the same on Holy Thursday (even though there is undoubtedly much joy then) because of the other events of Holy Week: the Lord's Passion and Death leading to his Easter Resurrection.

63

from a favorite prayer book or pray a decade of the rosary.

"Or maybe you forget what you are doing and simply gaze at the ceiling or at the windows, or look at the people around you. Perhaps you are one of the small number who leave the church after communion, before the final prayer and blessing.

"A very wise person and spiritual guide offers this advice on what to do after communion: 'When you return to your place, look around you, especially at the faces of others who are receiving the Eucharist.'

"Does this advice shock you, confuse you, leave you uncomfortable? Do you wonder how it can possibly be all right to look around after communion? Do you doubt whether it's really prayerful?

"Consider this: the Eucharist is more than a personal experience - which it surely can be and is. It is also, and above all, a community experience. Try to imagine the first Eucharistic celebration, the Last Supper. Jesus says to his closest friends and followers, 'This is my body; this is my blood. Take and eat; take and drink.' What a moment of mystery and wonder that must have been! Surely they did not bow their heads in silent isolation from one another on that occasion. Surely they did not have prayer books and rosaries in those days and no hymnals and organ music in the background. So what would their response have been?

"Imagine them, if you will, as a group with close ties. They had shared many high moments and many low moments. They cared for each other and for Jesus, their teacher. They had gathered to celebrate the family and community feast, the Passover. Here they are, sharing peace and fellowship and well-being, when Jesus does and says something they never expect. They are filled with awe and are drawn even closer. They gaze at him, unable to speak. They look at one another and their glances tell of wonder and love.

"When we prayerfully look at the faces of others returning from Holy Communion, we affirm once again that Jesus Christ lives in each of them as well as in ourselves. We can realize more fully that Christ goes out into the world in each one, no matter what their race, nationality, family, life, occupation, age. Each person becomes the Eucharist in the world, in school, in the workplace, in the home; with the sick, with the lonely, with the hurting; with the hungry, with the poor, with the unemployed.

"When we look into the faces of those who carry Eucharist within, perhaps that is the best prayer of all, for we are praying to the Living Lord who dwells within each of our brothers and sisters, and who with us are the BODY OF CHRIST."

A Side Street Thought

Please read the following statement
from the National Conference of Catholic
Bishops. The Bishops have shown a very sin-
cere and compassionate respect for all
Christians or others who feel drawn to the
Eucharist. As you read the statement, see
the theology behind it, and also feel some
of the pain of separation this statement
expresses.

Guidelines for Receiving Communion

For Catholics
Catholics fully participate in the
celebration of the Eucharist when they receive Holy Communion in fulfillment of
Christ's command to eat his Body and drink
his Blood. In order to be properly disposed
to receive Communion, communicants should
not be conscious of having committed grave
sin, have fasted for an hour, and seek to
live in charity and love with their neigh-
bors. Persons conscious of having committed
grave sin must first be reconciled with God
and the Church through the sacrament of
Penance. A frequent reception of the sacrament of Penance is encouraged for all.

For Other Christians
We welcome to this celebration of the

Eucharist those Christians who are not fully united with us. It is a consequence of the sad divisions in Christianity that we cannot extend to them a general invitation to receive communion. Catholics believe that the Eucharist is an action of the celebrating community signifying a oneness in faith, life, and worship of the community. Reception of the Eucharist by Christians not fully united with us would imply a oneness which does not yet exist, and for which we must all pray.

For Those Not Receiving Communion
Those not receiving sacramental communion are encouraged to express in their hearts a prayerful desire for unity with the Lord Jesus and with one another.

For Non-Christians
We also welcome to this celebration those who do not share our faith in Jesus. While we cannot extend to them an invitation to receive communion, we do invite them to be united with us in prayer.
                                                    NCCB

Why not pray for unity each and every time you share in the Eucharist? Do so as frequently and fully as possible.

At the International Charismatic Conference in Rome, there was a prophecy which rang with amazing force and power through St. Peter's Basilica: "The Body of my Son

67

is broken." That's still true today. The Body of God's Son _is_ still broken and that is why we need statements similar to that of the U.S. Bishops. It's time to renew our efforts for unity and where else shall we start but at the altar/table of the Lord where we are fed and nourished?

Does all that seem like a big job to you? Like it's an order from the big boss? Read on, MacDuff.

And That's An Order

"Our second grade Saturday morning catechism class was discussing the seven sacraments. With great difficulty they were able to name six of them and describe their purpose. But Holy Orders baffled them until irrepressible Colin had an inspiration. 'I know, I know,' he shouted in his haste to beat everyone to the 'obvious' answer. 'It's the Ten Commandments.'"*

---

*Story told by R.E. Walsh in "Catholic Digest, November 1989, p. 63.

CHAPTER SEVEN

THOUGHTS ON EUCHARISTIC DEVOTIONS AND OTHER TOPICS

"Bring it all back" is my approach to this particular subject. Our church communities are impoverished because we have given up many of the Eucharistic devotions. In the United States especially and in our big urban and suburban parishes in particular, there are so many activities, such a plethora of meetings, that one almost fears to schedule a Holy Hour or Forty Hours or Benediction of the Blessed Sacrament. That's not a good situation. These are all venerable and blessed practices and devotions. We need to treasure and use them, not trash and abuse them.

Maintain The Connection

The Church has very strongly directed us to maintain and proclaim quite clearly the organic connection between any and all of these devotions and the Eucharistic celebration. We are to be conscious of the central role that the Mass plays in our daily lives, so when we do come together to worship the Lord at a Holy Hour, during Forty Hours or Benediction, we are pro-

69

claiming a direct connection with the sacrifice of the Mass.

Always keeping that in mind, I think we need to use tremendous imagination and ingenuity to revive these Eucharistic devotions in our parish churches. I am not necessarily suggesting that the whole parish will flock to any of them, but there will always be some people who come. And there will always be Jesus.

What An Example!

It is interesting, however, that at St. James Church in Medjugorje where Our Lady is said to be appearing, adults, young adults and teenagers are experiencing an almost unbelievable revival of interest in the Mass. They gather each day to have Mass in their own language and often return in the evening for Mass in Croatian and Latin with certain sections in several languages. They pray the rosary together each day, spend hours in quiet prayer before the Blessed Sacrament, and eagerly seek out the sacrament of confession.

At almost any hour of the day (and many hours of the night) you will find them praying and saying the rosary on Apparition Hill, the place where Our Lady Queen of Peace is said to have first appeared.

This is not a gathering of older

people who have nothing else to do. This is
a gathering of all ages, the young and the
old and the middleaged also. And wonder of
wonders, the <u>young</u> and <u>young adults</u> are
there in numbers so strong that they often
outnumber their elders. This is a gathering
of people who have chosen to be there,
spending enormous amounts of time in prayer, in fasting, and in sharing their faith
lives.

Our Own Experience

The staff of the Sacred Heart Institute has found a similar hunger for the
Eucharist, though in smaller numbers. These
people delight in some of the traditional
Eucharistic devotions. On our retreats and
workshops, every afternoon is devoted to
quiet time before the Blessed Sacrament.

We preach balance in one's daily life
and try to promote it during our retreat
experience. During the afternoon free time
we encourage people to take a rest, get
some fresh air, and - most important - to
spend an hour before the Blessed Sacrament
exposed in the monstrance. We have experienced the results that come from such practices. Our evening Eucharistic celebrations
are always much more powerful when the participants have been energized and revital-
ized, have been loved and healed by quiet
time with their Eucharistic Lord and
friend.

Respect For The Eucharist

There used to be a venerable custom of tipping one's hat or making some other sign of reverence to the Blessed Sacrament when passing a church. In the book The Cardinal there is a beautiful description of how a motorman on a trolley car would tip his hat and say a special prayer every time he passed a church. When I pass a church I bless my forehead, my lips, and my heart and ask the Lord to be in a special way the Master of all my senses and being. Be Lord of my head (my will, my intellect, my memory, my imagination), my lips (all the means of communication that I have, verbal and non-verbal). The signing of my heart with his cross signifies the consecration of all my emotions to the Lord. "Jesus, be Lord of my feelings, my emotions. Let my heart be yours. I ask that you reign in my heart and take your place upon the throne in my heart. May no one else be Lord of my heart and lips and head but you. "For you alone are the Holy One. You alone are the Lord. You alone are the Most High, Jesus Christ, with the Holy Spirit in the glory of God the Father."

Please use this gesture if you like and even borrow my words until you begin to use your own. The greatest compliment you pay a teacher, preacher, or healer is to learn so well that eventually you make the subject your own and develop your own special approach. Enjoy every moment of this exciting discovery. Hope and blessings, joy and peace are in the journeying, not at the end, although no one would deny the beauty there.

There are difficulties, however, and one is highlighted very beautifully in the Broadway play "My Fair Lady" when Liza sings, "Words, words, words, I am so sick of words." The words and gestures are good because there is the grace of God moving us to utter those words or to make the gestures. But something else must happen.

We need openness to the grace of God, a willingness to follow the Lord, to put our money, lives, and our beings, where our mouths are. Yes, do say the words, make the gesture and then, with God's grace, do the actions of love. "Doing the actions of love" is from AA literature and means that no matter how I feel or what is going on, I decide to do the loving thing. And even if I have to grit my teeth, I do it with God's help, of course. I decide to follow the Lord and that's that.

Lord Jesus, you have heard all the words which can ever be uttered. You have seen all our pious, reverent, meaningful gestures and you wait for the actions of love. You wait for us to put our lives and our beings where our mouths are. But I have not been very good at doing that in the past. Please, help me and show me how.

Strengthen me that I may be able to do it in the future. Without you, Lord, I can do nothing. But the other side of that coin is a beautiful, consoling truth that with you all things are possible. With you obstacles can be overcome. With you, my God, we will win out. With you, though everything <u>seems</u> to end in defeat, there is no defeat. <u>With you</u> and <u>in you</u> and <u>through you</u> is the victory. Praise to you, Lord Jesus Christ. Thank you, Lord God Almighty.

Benediction

The service of Benediction is an old and beautiful one combining readings, song, and prayer. Candles, gleaming monstrance, rich vestments, music, incense, and - above all - the majestic real presence of our Lord in the Blessed Sacrament create a rich blend to delight our physical as well as our spiritual senses.

During Exposition of the Blessed Sacrament, we often sing this or a similar hymn.

<u>O Saving Victim</u>

O saving Victim op'ning wide
The gate of heav'n to us below!
Our foes press on from ev'ry side;
Thine aid supply, thy strength bestow.

74

To thy great name be endless praise.
Immortal Godhead, one in three;
Oh, grant us endless length of days
In our true native land with thee.
Amen.

As we adore the Lord in his Eucharistic Presence, there should be prayers, songs and readings to direct our attention. They may be readings from Scripture, a homily which develops a better understanding of the Eucharistic mystery, and time for silent prayer and reflection. The usual hymn at Benediction is the "Tantum Ergo." Its English translation is given here.

Tantum Ergo

Bowing low, then, offer homage
to a Sacrament so great!
Here is new and perfect worship;
All the old must terminate.
Senses cannot grasp this marvel;
Faith must serve to compensate.

Praise and glorify the Father,
Bless his Son's life-giving name,
Singing their eternal Godhead,
Power, majesty and fame.
Offering their Holy Spirit
Equal worship and acclaim. Amen.

At this point there is a beautiful sung or spoken dialogue between the priest or deacon and the people.

Presider: You have given them Bread from Heaven. (At Eastertime: Alleluia.)

People: Having within it all sweetness. (At Eastertime: Alleluia.)

Presider: Lord Jesus Christ, you gave us the Eucharist as the memorial of your suffering and death. May our worship of this sacrament of your body and blood help us to experience the salvation you won for us and the peace of the kingdom where you live with the Father and the Holy Spirit, one God, forever and ever. Amen.

Then the priest puts on the humeral veil and goes to the altar, genuflects and picks up the monstrance very lovingly and carefully, wrapping the veil around its base.

Next he blesses the congregation. At some services, particularly at Marian shrines (Lourdes, etc.), the priest, bishop, or deacon goes to each of the sick people present (many on stretchers) and blesses them individually. I have done something similar on retreats, either blessing people one at a time or in small groups when those groups have been meeting and praying together for the weekend.

After the blessing the priest puts the monstrance back on the altar, removes the humeral veil, and then kneels before the Lord. Together he and the people say:

The Divine Praises

Blessed be God.
Blessed be his holy name.
Blessed be Jesus Christ, true God and true man.
Blessed be the name of Jesus.
Blessed be his most Sacred Heart.
Blessed be his most precious blood.
Blessed be Jesus in the most holy sacrament of the altar.
Blessed be the Holy Spirit, the Paraclete.
Blessed be the great mother of God, Mary most holy.
Blessed be her holy and immaculate conception.
Blessed be her glorious assumption.
Blessed be the name of Mary, virgin and mother.
Blessed be Saint Joseph, her most chaste spouse.
Blessed be God in his angels and in his saints.

Afterward a most beautiful prayer is often recited.

May the heart of Jesus, in the most Blessed Sacrament, be praised, adored, and loved with grateful affection, at every moment, in all the tabernacles of the world, even to the end of time. Amen.

A final hymn is sung, often "Holy God, We Praise Thy Name." The people leave or stay on for a while, but in either case, something imperceivable has happened. There is a greater sense of serenity.

When you next participate in this lovely devotion, notice how you and the other "Catholics who can't sing like their Protestant brothers and sisters" suddenly find your voices and sing with gusto the "golden oldies" and even some of the newer hymns. "Ab esse ad posse valet elatio" is a Latin expression (I've gotten better since my days as an altar boy!) and it means "If it has been done then it's quite valid to say it can be done." If we sing so well at Benediction and at Christmas time, then we can sing. It just takes more effort on our parts and some prudence on the part of Directors of Music/Organists. They too often change the hymns before we've learned the words and long before we've learned to like them and finally treasure them.

Forty Hours Devotion And Processions

Andrew Greeley has said in one of his T.V. appearances that when the Catholic

Church discards something then the world picks it up. We gave up, to a large extent, incense and rosary beads; and the hippies started using them. We gave up holy hours, Forty Hours, and processions to honor Jesus or Mary and our own people turned to Eastern gurus who promised to teach them how to meditate and pray. And various groups took to the streets in huge marches to promote civil rights, pro or anti-life movements, and dozens of other issues. Read the following, please, and take some time to reflect on it.*

"On Corpus Christi procession day in Port Harcourt, Nigeria, Africa, the road of peace was made from St. Mary's Cathedral to St. Philip's parish. We prayed for peace. God sent rain. The people danced and sang in the rain.

In the falling rain and steady wind, I pressed on, praying, listening, seeing and learning of the <u>power</u> <u>of</u> <u>Jesus</u> <u>Christ</u> <u>to</u> <u>start</u> <u>and</u> <u>move</u> <u>people</u>. It was the first time I recall the Blessed Sacrament being carried into the place of Benediction to the sound of resounding cheering and clap-

---

*"Where the Church is Booming" by Bishop Edmund Fitzgibbon of Port Harcourt, Nigeria. From "Catholic Digest," October 1987, pp. 7-8.

ping. Everyone was drenched. No one thought of seeking shelter. Judges, lawyers, doctors, mothers, children stood their ground as if nothing was happening except the Eucharist. I have not seen anything like it before, here or anywhere else."

"Let's bring it all back" is still my thought, but let's not wait for the Pope. He's pretty clear on what he wants. Let's do what we can to promote devotion to the Eucharist; and let's join with others who are working for this cause. And, for God's sake and the Church's, reach out to others who are older or younger. It can happen if we make the effort.

Spiritual Communion

If for some reason you are not able to receive Communion at Mass, the church encourages you to make an act of spiritual Communion. The individual who is unable to receive because he or she has already received twice that day (or for whatever reason) expresses a hunger and longing for communion with the Lord in words of the heart, mind, and possibly the lips. A sample of such a prayer is included here.

My Jesus, I believe that you are present in the Blessed Sacrament. I love you above all things and I desire you in my soul. Since I cannot now receive you sacramentally, come at least spiritually into my heart. As though you were already there, I embrace you and unite myself wholly to you; permit not that I should ever be separated from you.

There is a variation on spiritual communion which several people recommend. Wherever you are and whatever the circumstances (trial, temptation, emotional upheaval, etc.), turn physically as much as possible toward the nearest church and let your mind and heart reach out in adoration and praise to the Lord present in the Blessed Sacrament.

Ask him for the specific help you need at that time. Then thank him for all his many gifts of love to you over your whole lifetime. Draw from him whatever grace or strength you need at that moment. Ask the Lord to pour his love and light and healing power into you and any other person who is part of the situation. Breathe in his peace and his healing love. Let it so envelop you that it is almost like a soft gentle shower, what the Irish call "a fine sort of day" which fills the atmosphere with moisture without violence or pyrotechnics.

AA's Big Book recommends that when a person is hungry, angry, lonely, or tired (HALT) he or she needs to be very careful. At such times it's suggested that one pause and breathe deeply of the presence of the Higher Power. After a short time, say quietly but with great sincerity the Serenity Prayer, which appears elsewhere in this book but which is certainly worth repeating.

> God, grant me the <u>Serenity</u> to accept the things I cannot change;
> <u>Courage</u> to change the things I can; and
> <u>Wisdom</u> to know the difference.

I've tried both - an act of spiritual communion and the Serenity prayer. They work! Whatever one appeals to you, use it. In fact, I don't think anyone would be offended if you combined both of them as I often do.

I'm convinced that Jesus Christ is the Lord of my life. I pray to know him better each day. I cannot presume that I am always going to allow him to be Lord. I must continually fight a battle with my <u>urge</u> to control every situation- to be the master of my own fate. In fact, the battle with self is a constant one.

At times you may have to admit your own lack of control and turn to the Lord deliberately and completely. Believe me, that's a very difficult thing to do. We have to admit our need for a power greater than ourselves to get us out of the mess we have made of our lives and back onto the right road. As far as I'm concerned, the only one who can do that is the Lord Jesus

Christ. But each person has to come to that understanding and acceptance in his or her own time.

Our Lady of the Blessed Sacrament

Our Lady of the Most Blessed Sacrament was the name of the parish at which I worshipped in grade school and at Seton Hall Prep. I was already thinking about studying for the priesthood because the pastor (the one I assisted when I served my first Mass) took a great interest in me. He was an austere man, very forbidding on the outside, but a warm and concerned individual underneath. His friendship and affection tied me even more closely to the parish and to the title of Our Lady which it bore. Later on we moved to Blessed Sacrament parish in Newark, and eventually I spent almost a year of my priesthood at Our Lady of the Most Blessed Sacrament in Roseland, NJ.

Mother Of My Vocation

Reflecting on all this confirms my suspicion that Our Lady of the Blessed Sacrament has been watching over my vocation from the very moment of its inception. I will be surprised if, when I reach heaven (and I fully expect to do so), she doesn't confirm it absolutely.

Someone once asked me about her title as Our Lady of the Blessed Sacrament. The answer seemed so obvious. She is Mother of the Lord Jesus Christ and his body the Church. She bore Jesus in her womb and gave him to the world at the first Christmas. She was so much a part of the early church that I'm sure she delighted in their agapes at which the Eucharist was celebrated. She was cared for by John and loved him dearly. So she would definitely have shared in the Eucharist with him and many of the first followers of her son.

If there were no churches named "Our Lady of the Blessed Sacrament" I would want to know why not. She is so obviously a part of this great mystery of her Son's love for her and all of us.

It seems to me that Our Lady must take great delight when we her children attend daily Mass and/or visit her son in the Blessed Sacrament. Her great maternal heart must delight when we, in response to his call and his grace, come to be with him in a special way. Why not ask her for her help so that you too will answer the call that is always there to come to daily Mass and to any other Eucharistic devotions your church might offer?

The Eucharist and St. Therese of Lisieux

Saints are our sisters and brothers in the Lord who have achieved the final heal-ing: life eternal with him. Let's consider some things which one saint said about the Eucharist.

Therese of Lisieux lived in a time when Catholics only rarely received communion, but she knew what a terrible loss that was. Therese wrote to her cousin who was visiting the world exhibition in Paris: "Jesus burns with desire to come into your heart as your heart is made to love Jesus, to love him passionately . . . Receive communion often, very often."

Therese recognized that the Eucharist is the bread of life and bread is to be eaten. "Our Lord does not come just to be left waiting for long periods of time in a golden tabernacle. He comes to be taken into the living temple of our hearts." St. Therese received communion frequently. It made a saint of her. It can do the same for each of us.

When speaking of the first time she received the Lord in the Eucharist, she recalled, "I knew that I was loved and I, in my turn, told him that I loved him and was giving myself to him . . ." Something had melted away and there were no longer two of them. Jesus only was left. Therese felt united once and for all with divine love.

As I've said previously, that was not my experience the first time I received, but I'm not giving up. Slowly but surely I'm getting there, and I'm only in my middle fifties so there's still time for me. If you're younger, you are even better off. If you're older than I, there's still time. But why not put some more effort and prayer, fasting and good works into your preparation for communion?

I Have Been Touched

At my first Communion, as I've indicated, I was not too taken up with the tremendous Present I had just received. I am not one of the great saints and I guess a lot of people aren't either because their first Communions never made an indelible impression on them.

However, I've been at other first Communions which touched me deeply. Watching some of my nephews and nieces and even some of their children receive has helped me to appreciate the Eucharist more and has moved me to receive Communion more fervently with them.

I've celebrated the Eucharist as the pastor of a parish and rejoiced as the girls and boys came to the altar with their parents to receive Communion for the first time. I've seen the joy and the wonder in the eyes of the children. But I've also seen something very special in the eyes of the parents and the grandparents. It really has been a family celebration and, again, it helped renew my appreciation of the Eucharist.

There is a tremendous leakage in our Church. People decide they will no longer worship with us and "retire" or drop out of our parishes. Often this happens when they are in their late teens or early twenties. Some of them have come back to the church. But it's not enough.

You Can Touch Many!

We can't become complacent about the numbers that return while so many stay away. Such "retired" or inactive Catholics may come back when they have their first child, or at that child's Baptism. Many of them seem to return to the sacramental life of the church when their children receive First Communion. It behooves us to make such occasions very special. We need to involve the parents in the preparation and the celebration.

Our parishes, especially the priests and catechetical people, need to involve the parents in the preparation and celebration. We must be available to them and let them know we care. Let's be very clear about our desire to see them be an active part of the community.

At Holy Trinity in Westfield, we had three separate celebrations. Only a reasonably small number of children received, and they were surrounded by parents and family, relatives and friends. Each celebration had a huge congregation and was a real family gathering and celebration.

The Sunday following the celebration of First Communion was reserved for a Mass for the children, their families, and as many other parishioners as we could get there. Each child was given a special award and blessing, and was encouraged to "Come Back" each Sunday to be with us - their family in Christ. We always found that the families and others there sat up and took notice whenever we spoke to the children. The little child in each of them responded. No matter how nonchalant they looked, their ears came to life in an unusually receptive mode.

When you attend the celebration of First Communion think about these observations. If you are a practicing Catholic and committed Christian, then you may be able to reach out and touch some inactive Catholics and lead them back to the Church. So often people feel barred from the sacraments because of being in a second marriage or being divorced. When all the facts are known, there may be no real problem. Encourage them to talk with a priest, deacon or pastoral associate.

Be clear about what is important to you in the Eucharist. Be awake and aware and you can and will help others to a deeper understanding of the Eucharist.

Prayer

Lord Jesus, thank you for being persistent and everlastingly compassionate. Thank you for calling me to my First Communion and all the other times I have received you. Please, Lord, help me to grow in my love of you in the Eucharist and especially in Communion. Never let me take you for granted, nor our brothers and sisters who are intimately joined with us at that time. And, Lord Jesus, bless the little children of the world - and the not so little ones also.

CHAPTER EIGHT

SOUL STIRRING HYMNS AND PRAYERS

A Parable

Once upon a time there was a poor, simple, humble parish priest who was feeling very tense and yet depressed. What could he do? Then he received two gifts which helped him. The first was a set of audio cassette tapes: "Give Thanks" and "All Hail, King Jesus." The second was a prayer he had learned years before, but now its words sprang to life again: "Lord Jesus Christ, bridge the gap between the love I needed and the love I received."

You may have guessed, I am that priest. Please, permit me to share with you what these two gifts mean to me.

A Gift Of Song

The two tapes contained many songs of praise. In my room and car, in most of my spare moments, I played them. They became a special part of my day and helped me through many a tense moment.

91

When on the road and forced to spend weary hours in the car, I played them. Often I sang along and at first I used to wonder what the other drivers might be thinking, but it quickly dawned on me that they weren't that interested in what I was doing, and why in the world should I worry about what they were thinking?

The weary hours in the car were lightened immensely by these songs. The distances were still the same, but they seemed to speed by. It was a wonderful experience to rediscover how praising and adoring the Lord is such a gift. It was a gift to me, but it was also a lovely gift to God.

These songs began to be the background music of my life. Many times I would wake with snatches of them in my mind. Other times I would catch myself singing or humming them in spare moments or when walking through the halls. Words of praise flashed into my mind and heart at the most amazing times. Often when counseling a person, part of one of the songs would be just what the doctor (God) ordered for that person.

A Gift Of Understanding

Only much later did it dawn on me that the words which I had been listening to, proclaiming and praying, had indeed become not only a part of my day and life, but were literally coming true right before my eyes. Jehovah, God my provider, was taking care of all my needs and my parish's also. Jehovah was healing me in new and deeper ways.

I had just spent several weeks concentrating on raising funds for the various ministries of the Institute. And suddenly everything began to fall into place. It was true. God had provided for our needs. God had again healed my insecurities and doubts and lack of confidence in him. And that was my greatest need.

I had to remind myself who was the pastor of the parish and the President, C.E.O., etc. of the Institute. Jesus was and is in charge. It's his parish, his Institute, and he will provide for it. (Robert Schuler once remarked on his TV service that God normally is quite economical in his ways. He provides the vision. Then he expects us to begin to work to achieve that vision. As we do so, moving out in faith and trust, he begins to supply all the rest of our needs.)

The praise tapes were a gift of encouragement. They hit me right between the eyes. In a way it was a more subtle version of the famous chiropractor's method of helping horses. He uses a baseball bat and a two by four to adjust them. Anything less would never penetrate their tough hides.

I realized that I had been thick-headed and obstinate, although much less so than a horse. So God in his gentleness decided to penetrate my heart, mind and will and every other place by saturating me with music and song, with praise and worship.

A Gift Of Prayer

The second gift was not new, but I had placed it in a category entitled, "I'll save that for someone who comes to me for help." It did work that way and one of my parishioners left the rectory thanking God for the "kind and compassionate priest" who had just helped him rediscover God's love through a wonderful prayer. A few hours later it struck me most forcefully that I needed that prayer even more than the parishioner did. "Lord Jesus Christ, bridge the gap between the love I needed and the love I received. Be the bridge over the gap between the love I need and the love I am receiving."

So much a part of my being has that prayer become that it too has become part of the background music of my existence. I often wake and sleep with that on my mind. It also is with me during the day and night while driving, working, resting, and meeting with people. "Lord Jesus Christ, bridge the gap between the love _we_ needed and the love _we_ received."

Some Reflections

Notice how that prayer is so flexible, referring to the past or present. We need never take ourselves out of the prayer as we always say it for the love _we_ needed, the love _we_ received.

You may be wondering how this story on gifts fits in with the Eucharist. Well, let me share with you how I implement its lesson.

As I celebrate and preside at the Eucharist, and in my quiet moments of adoration, the words of those tapes and of that very special prayer have filtered through my mind and sprung to my lips.

Saturation

Brothers and sisters, what I am talking about here is saturation. We need to be saturated and enveloped in such gifts and other gifts of healing the Lord has given us. Too often in my own life what I have done is to say, "Oh, that's really good." Then I use whatever it is for a time and store it away for when I can use it to help someone the Lord sends to me. How slow I am to realize that I am that person and I need to grow in love for myself and to apply these gifts of healing to my life and work. I need to acknowledge the deep and, at times, desperate need for healing in my life.

Again, we are talking about saturation of our entire being. These are not healing gifts I draw upon when I am under attack. These are the mainstays of my life, _its background music_. They spring to the fore when I am under attack from the inside or the outside because they are my ordinary equipment and part of my very being. These songs and this prayer help me to celebrate the Eucharist in a more healing way; and on the other hand, the Eucharistic setting gives them a power they'd never have alone.

I know a priest who is a joyful recovering alcoholic (and believe me he is all of the above in spades and has a fruitful and blessed ministry to many of God's people). Once I asked him to explain the AA practice of going to "ninety meetings in ninety days." "That's part of the wisdom of the program," he answered. "It came out of our experience of how to _get_ and _stay_ sober but also to grow in our recovery."

"Ninety meetings in ninety days" means saturation. Gradually, the wisdom of the program, the sobriety displayed by its members, the companionship offered by one's sponsor and others begin to soak in and help a person _get_ and _stay_ sober. This is rarely an instantaneous thing. It is an intensive crash course in sober living. Any addict, no matter what his or her social position, background, finances, culture and education, needs that crash course in order to stay alive.

What we have been talking about is quite similar. We seek saturation of our total being with praise and worship, prayer and God's love. That's a healing program that works. And the Eucharist - Mass and quiet time before the Blessed Sacrament (hopefully often, if not daily) - is the mainstay and <u>sine qua non</u> for us.

Soul Stirring Hymns

In the seminary of the Immaculate Conception of the Archdiocese of Newark in the late 50's one of the seminarians would sing "Panis Angelicus" (the Bread of Angels) on very special occasions. He had a magnificent voice, and the chapel would still in anticipation as he began.

At my 25th anniversary as a priest in May of 1985, one of the Dominican sisters of Caldwell, New Jersey, sang "Panis Angelicus" as the Communion meditation. She sang with a different quality and a different style than the seminarian over twenty-five years ago, but with a force and a beauty and a penetrating quality that brought tears to many eyes. Obviously that's an all time favorite for many people. It certainly is for me.

The words are important and we'll look at them soon. But the words are not so important as the wealth of memories and images, soul-stirring and also "gentle breeze" moments associated with this hymn.

The Eucharist is truly the bread of angels, panis angelicus, but not in the way it is the bread of all humans. The angels worship and adore the Lord in the Eucharist, but we are given the great grace of sharing in this wonderful banquet. The angels watch and wonder at the Lord's complete gift of himself. They delight in those times when we are most aware of the treasure we have offered to us.

Sister Lucia, sole survivor of the three children of Fatima, says that while they were in a pasture an angel appeared to them for the third time,* "holding in his hands a chalice surmounted by a Host, from which drops of blood were falling. Eventually after offering prayers of adoration and reparation, the angel gave the Host to Lucia and the contents of the chalice to Jacinta and Francisco, saying at the same

---

*Lucia Speaks, AMI Press, Washington, NJ, p. 16. "Most Holy Trinity, Father , Son and Holy Spirit, I adore Thee profoundly. I offer Thee the most precious Body, Blood, Soul and Divinity of Jesus Christ, present in all the tabernacles of the world, in (continued on page 99)

time: 'Take and drink the Body and Blood of Jesus Christ, horribly outraged by ungrateful men. Repair their crimes and console your God.'"

Another Eucharistic hymn is "O Sacrum Convivium." This means "O sacred life-giving meal." How true it is that the Eucharist is so much more than an ordinary meal. It is a life-renewing and enhancing banquet which gives joy and happiness in the companionship of the Lord who is the answer to all our needs.

Prayers Before And After Communion

The Church has a treasury of prayers from centuries gone by and yet few of us comprehend the vastness of these riches. I am resisting the urge to include many prayers to be used before and after Communion. Only a few are suggested here because you can easily find books which contain others. One of these prescribed here will, I trust, speak to your heart. Begin to use it frequently if not daily as it's for you to pray now and not later.

---

reparation for the outrages, sacrileges and indifference by which He is offended. And through the infinite merits of His most Sacred Heart, and of the Immaculate Heart of Mary, I beg the conversion of poor sinners."

Write Your Own

Perhaps you will begin to speak to the Lord directly in your own words. In fact, I challenge you to compose a prayer of your own. Literally what I am suggesting is that you write the words down, no matter how simple or awkward they feel. Then continue to work with your prayer, use it and rearrange it until it expresses what you feel. Then it will be truly yours. You will own it and feel about it in a way no other prayer can match. Any effort you put into this endeavor will be abundantly blessed.

A Sampler For You!

These are the prayers I suggest and before each one there is a short comment. You may want to pray the prayer out loud (after your first reading). Write them down, if you like, on a piece of paper which you will carry with you in your pocket, wallet, or purse. The idea is to use them to grow in your love for such a loving and prodigal God.

Before Mass:

Offering Of The Holy Mass

Accept, Most Holy Trinity, this sacrifice fulfilled at one time by the Divine Word and now renewed on this altar by the hands of your priest. I unite myself to the intentions of Jesus Christ, Priest and Victim, that I may be entirely offered for your glory and for the salvation of all. I intend through Jesus Christ, with Jesus Christ, and in Jesus Christ to adore your eternal majesty, to thank your immense goodness, to satisfy your offended justice, and to beseech your mercy for the church, for my dear ones, and for myself.

While waiting to receive Communion:

The priest or deacon usually says this prayer quietly while the sacred vessels are being cleaned. I think it's a beautiful prayer before receiving.

"Lord, may I receive these gifts in purity of heart. May they bring me healing and strength now and forever."

I wrote/composed this prayer because I did not find any one I liked. Feel free to change it.

O Lord, I am not worthy to receive you. Touch me in my unworthiness and calm me, heal me, and love me into deeper repentance and conversion. Say but the Word. Be but the Word which heals me in body, mind and spirit. I belong to you and I hunger and yearn for you in Communion. May your Mother and my Mother, all the

angels and saints and all my loved ones
accompany me as I come forward to receive
you in Communion. My heart is ready, O
Lord. I am yours!

After Communion

Anima Christi

Soul of Christ, sanctify me. Body of
Christ, save me. Blood of Christ, inebriate
me. Water from the side of Christ, wash me.
Passion of Christ, strengthen me. O good
Jesus, hear me. Within your wounds hide me.
Suffer me not to be separated from you.
From the malignant enemy defend me. In the
hour of my death, call me and bid me come
to you, that with your saints I may praise
you forever and ever. Amen.

After Mass

Prayer of St. Thomas Aquinas, O.P.

Lord, Father all powerful and ever-
living God, I thank you, for even though I
am a sinner, your unprofitable servant, not
because of my worth, but in the kindness of
your mercy, you have fed me with the precious body and blood of your Son, our Lord
Jesus Christ. I pray that this holy communion may not bring me condemnation and pun-
ishment, but forgiveness and salvation. May
it be a helmet of faith and a shield of

good will. May it purify me from evil ways
and put an end to my evil passions. May it
bring me charity and patience, humility and
obedience and growth in the power to do
good. May it be my strong defense against
all my enemies, visible and invisible and
the perfect calming of all my evil impul-
ses, bodily and spiritual. May it unite me
more closely to you, the one true God, and
lead me safely through death to everlasting
happiness with you. And I pray that you
will lead me, a sinner, to the banquet
where you, with your Son and Holy Spirit,
are true and perfect light, total fulfillment, everlasting joy, gladness without
end, and perfect happiness to your saints.
Grant this through Christ our Lord. Amen .

Prayer To Jesus Christ Crucified

My good and dear Jesus, I kneel before
you, asking you most earnestly to engrave
upon my heart a deep and lively faith,
hope, and charity, with true repentance for
my sins, and a firm resolve to make amends.
As I reflect upon your five wounds, and
dwell upon them with deep compassion and
grief, I recall, good Jesus, the words the
prophet David spoke long ago concerning
yourself: they have pierced my hands and my
feet, they have counted all my bones!

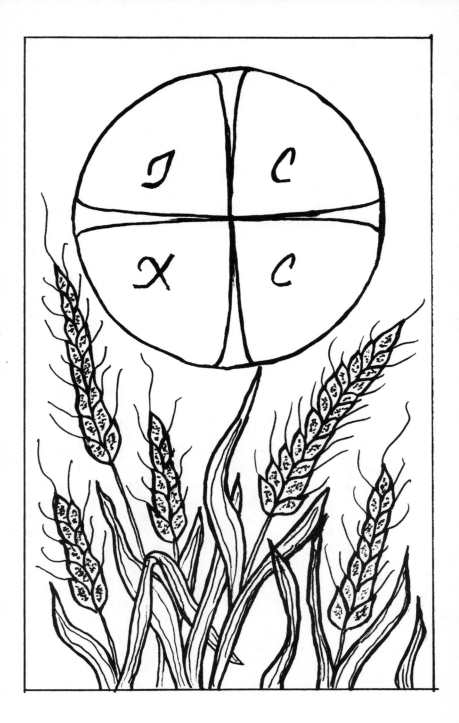

CHAPTER NINE

PRACTICES: GOOD AND BAD

While studying at Manhattan College one summer, I was stopped by a woman who asked me, "Are you coming to the underground Mass?" "Where is it being held?" I asked. "On the top floor of the dorm building." I nearly collapsed on the grass in gales of laughter. Not at the person, but at the concept of having an underground Mass on the top floor of a building.

Her invitation (which I politely declined) was to an "experimental" Mass where the priest used no vestments, no unleavened bread, and made up his own Eucharistic prayer. Such innovations were quite the rage at that time.

I don't hear those terms too much any more, and I'm happy about that as I was never that thrilled with some of the innovations. It all seemed so faddish. I would prefer to celebrate the Eucharist in such a way that it is apparent that the Lord Jesus Christ is truly the priest, the victim, the Lamb of God, the bread of heaven, our Lord and Brother, our Healer and our Hope.

Many people have shared with me what were some meaningful Eucharistic celebrations. Few were <u>underground</u> Masses. Some talked about small group celebrations and mentioned how comfortable it was when fewer than ten people were there. One person remembers celebrating the Eucharist in her own home and feeling an intimacy and a community spirit there which moved her to joyful tears.

There are other times when a huge number of people gather for the Eucharist. In 1964 I concelebrated the closing Mass at the Eucharistic Congress in Bombay, India, at which 300,000 people had gathered. It was a magnificent celebration, and I was deeply honored to be the only priest from North America to participate. That particular celebration was filled with awe and wonder at the multitude of people present. The Eucharist had been the center of our lives for six days and now we were reaching the apex of the whole Congress. Jesus was truly Lord of our lives and energies and we proclaimed it fearlessly and clearly.

At one of the Eastern Regional Charismatic Conferences, we had a smaller but similar celebration. In 1978, 37,000 people participated in the closing Eucharist. What joy we felt. It was magnificent and the participation was outstanding. People were there and they wanted to celebrate!

When I'm concelebrating Mass at our

Cathedral or in other churches, I receive the Body and Blood of the Lord and then sit down. Don't tell the liturgists or musicians, but I most often turn off the singing and everything else and enter into a deep awareness of the Lord's presence. I delight in the gentle healing quiet time that I experience right after receiving Communion. My heart hungers for that and I do not often achieve it when celebrating Sunday Masses. There always seems to be so much going on that it is hard to get quiet. Yet, gradually, I have disciplined myself to take a minute or two of quiet time and encourage the people to do the same.

The Lord moves mightily in those moments as many have attested. Sister Ruthann recently told me of one experience she had after receiving Communion.

"I went back to my place and decided to take advantage of this healing time to give the Lord my list of things I'd like healed. I was busy yammering away at him when all at once I saw him, sitting on a throne. He was all dressed in white and he was very, very big. I was standing in front of him and suddenly I was a little girl, blonde braids and all with the kind of plaid taffeta ribbons on my braids that I always used to get to wear to church. Jesus reached down and picked me up. First he sat me on his lap and I became conscious of a great love. Then he put his hands on me again and lifted me up against his shoul-

der, the way we do with children. I just
stayed there with my arms around his neck.
There were no words, no sounds, just me and
Jesus loving each other. My "list" was for-
gotten. What I had received was more than
enough. The gap had been bridged."

I'm always amazed at how people decide
that as soon as they've received, it's out
the door, light up a cigarette, and start
to talk. They often are in no hurry as they
stay around to chat. That's an almost blas-
phemous attitude. Since we do believe that
the Eucharist is the Body and Blood of
Christ, our Savior and our Lord, our Friend
and our Brother, our Hope and our Healer,
then what are we doing slipping out of
church and running back into the arms of
the world? I cannot survive without the Eucharist. And I have had to proclaim again
and again to myself what is important and
who is important. Perhaps you need to do
something similar.

Some of the greatest saints and converts have come into the Church because of
the Eucharist. How often Jesus seems to
reach out from the Eucharistic celebration
and from the tabernacle to gather people
in. He is offering us the opportunity to do
the same in our own way. He is waiting and
he is hungering for people to come to him.
What puny efforts we often make to spread
Eucharistic love and devotion!

Why is it that many converts are so

much more enthusiastic than we? They are consumed with a hunger for the Lord Jesus Christ in the Eucharist. Do they know something we don't know? Not at all! Do they understand something we don't? What do you think?

Some signs on churches ask the question: "What's missing in CH__CH?" Obviously "U R." Are we missing the boat and letting a golden opportunity slip by for evangelization, for reaching out and helping people?

May this book call people back to their first fervor. May it energize them to reach out and share the good news we have been discussing. Don't tell people a lot. Let them guess and then ask you what's changed you.

If people do ask then tell them, "It's the Eucharist. It's not only a supper experience, but a super experience, and I can't get enough of it." Walk away then and let them think about your changed life and your words. Be on fire for the Lord in the Eucharist. Be consumed with a hunger for the Bread of Angels which has come down to feed us, and often share the sacred banquet of the Lord's table.

Let others note your attitude toward the Eucharist, and watch their reaction. Betcha they'll be back!

EPILOGUE

My Last Word, But Not The Lord's

The best way I have of thanking you for reading thus far is at the greatest Thanksgiving Service we have: The Eucharist. Edifying and consoling, strengthening and enabling are just a few words which inadequately describe my love for the great Lord who feeds and nourishes us each day at Mass. You and yours are remembered each time I celebrate the Eucharist. Remember me there also. Why not use these two prayer reflections?

How Blessed We Are

How blessed are we to have
    the Eucharist
    in our lives.
We are a people of
    the book and the cup.
    The Word of God is ours
        in the Bible and in his
        Body and Blood given for us
        to redeem us.
How truly fortunate we are to have
    gifts
    graces
    such as these at our disposal.

Lord Jesus, let me never take you for granted, nor neglect the magnificent gift you are to me. I don't ever want to leave you - God's greatest healing gift - too often unrecognized and unappreciated. Help me to live as your follower - one who values and is proud of the Book, the Bread, and the Chalice you have so generously given to me. Thank you now and forever. Amen.

More Valuable Than Any Jewel

The Eucharist is not a diamond nor
    a pearl
but bread
    nourishment
    life.
At times the setting may be
    wrong. But
    when it is right
what an extraordinary experience of
    Jesus
    our Eucharistic Lord and Healer!

O Lord of Love and Life, help us as your body, and individually as your followers, to discover you in each and every Eucharistic celebration we share.

+

Let's work at it. More important, let's relax into it.

SACRED
HEART
INSTITUTE

Suite 5C
585 Bloomfield Avenue
Caldwell, New Jersey 07006
201-226-7077

THE SACRED HEART INSTITUTE

Mission Statement

The Sacred Heart Institute, founded in June 1979, is a Christian center devoted to preaching, teaching, and healing. The center was run on a part-time basis by its founder Father Gerald P. Ruane from June 1979 until March 1981 when it was established as a program of Catholic Community Services of the Roman Catholic Archdiocese of Newark, New Jersey.

In 1986 it was transferred to the Directorate of Pastoral Services of the Archdiocese because the Institute began to focus on spiritual direction rather than clinical counseling.

The present and future thrust of the Institute is three-fold:

1) exploring in greater depth the healing of male and female self-identities;

2) further concentration on the area of grief and the healing power of the Christian community when confronted with people in the midst of the grieving process; and

3) the study and publicizing of the spirituality of the twelve-steps.

These three areas, it seems to us, are going to be of paramount concern to the Church in the 1990's. The Institute's emphasis will be on evangelizing the unchurched and the non-churched, fallen away and disillusioned Catholics. It has been the experience of the staff that there has been tremendous leakage from the Catholic Church and especially from our Catholic parishes. In the Archdiocese of Newark it is estimated that only 25% of the Catholic population attends weekend liturgies.

Since October 1989, many of our healing services, seminars, and workshops are being held at Our Lady of All Souls parish in East Orange, New Jersey. This is a city parish with an extraordinarily beautiful church and a small congregation. The parish and the Institute are working to "fill" that church and, in the long run, as many churches as possible.

These three areas of our concentration touch all people in the deepest part of their beings. People who are hurting because of grief, because of addiction, because of confusion about their self-identities either as male or female are seeking healing. They will go to almost any lengths to obtain it and that's why we feel that the Church has to muster its tremendous resources to bring healing into these areas.

It is our experience and deep conviction that people get reunited with ("recycled back into") the Church community as they get healed of their various addictions, wounds, and misconceptions. Evangelization is not an instantaneous event nor is healing. Both are evolutionary, on-going processes, requiring great staying power to bring this two-fold ministry to fruition.

Occasionally someone will have a deep conversion experience at a healing service or seminar, but the vast majority of times we have seen them slowly but surely going through the process of return. Quite frequently they are angry at the Church for real or perceived wrongs. Once they are able to receive loving compassionate attention, they soon move to seeking prayer for healing and then move on to reintegration into the Church, and begin to search for meaningful participation in their parish communities. The staff has experienced this in their ministry many times.

As people continue to seek spiritual direction and to develop very strong prayer lives, it is not unusual for some of them then to consider a religious or priestly vocation. Others seek to participate in the lay ministries of the church and often, if married, a couple may decide to join the Christian Family Movement. Not infrequently a couple may decide that the husband should become a candidate for the diaconate.

Healing is evangelization at the deepest core of an individual's being. This two-fold process takes time and effort. The Sacred Heart Institute is committed to a concerted and multi-faceted approach to both ends. We believe in ministering to the saved and to the good people of the parishes, but we also know the power of this ministry to touch the disaffected, the walking wounded, and even the often cynical and highly critical lapsed Catholics.

The Institute is like the proverbial and scriptural lilies of the field, depending upon the prayers and volunteer efforts of many people. Approximately half of the annual budget comes from the retreats and seminars sponsored by the Institute and its book and audio/video cassette ministry. The remainder comes from the donations of individuals and small groups, and grants from various foundations and corporations.

ABOUT THE AUTHOR

Rev. Gerald P. Ruane, Ph.D., a Roman Catholic priest, is presently on sabbatical during which he will be writing several books and articles and preaching and teaching in various parts of the United States and other countries.

He has most recently served as pastor of Holy Trinity parish in Westfield, New Jersey, while still serving as the Director of the Sacred Heart Institute of the Archdiocese of Newark, New Jersey.

Father Ruane has a doctorate in religious education and has studied at several schools in the United States as well as at the Catholic University of Louvain in Belgium and at Oxford University in England.

With this volume on the Eucharist, Father Ruane inaugurates a new series of books on healing. This series is entitled "The Greatest Healing Gifts." Future volumes will treat Jesus as the Healing Word of God in the Scriptures, and Jesus as he heals us by daily devotions.

This present volume is Father's fifth book. Previous books have discussed the topics of homiletics, Daily Homilies for the Year (1968); the theology of death, Birth to Birth: The Life-Death Mystery (1976); and healing, Overcoming Obstacles

<u>To</u> <u>Healing</u> (1985) and <u>Healing</u> <u>And</u> <u>Your</u> <u>Emo-</u>
<u>tional</u> <u>Life</u> (1986).

As Director of the Sacred Heart Institute, Father gives workshops and seminars,
retreats and lectures on preaching, teaching, and especially healing. He also celebrates Healing Masses.

He is a charter life-long member of
the Association of Christian Therapists.